NEVER STOP DANCING

NEVER STOP DANCING

by Toni Ortner

Editor Joseph Bruchac III

Originally published by Greenfield Review Press

Copyright © 1976, 2006 by Toni Ortner

ISBN: 978-1-5040-2922-3

Distributed in 2016 by Open Road Distribution
180 Maiden Lane
New York, NY 10038
www.openroadmedia.com

for all those locked inside

The black girl
in the padded cell next to me
beat the walls   screamed all night

no one cld shut

didn't care
how long
she was there

same inside or out

the rules broke her
now she was gonna break every fuckin rule
in the
place she didn't make

I wanted to get my razor back
when the sun came up
one with the nice sharp edges

made sure to walk past the
nurse's station

with a light high step
a clear cheerful whistle

they wrote down everything
everything went onto those charts

even the color of yr
piss

analyzed

rules even in there
stop   pass   proceed to go

get
out.

50   60   70   80   90
I am the engine
the Engineer is not here   sorry
he must have turned up the steam
pushed down the throttle   gone to sleep
keep on shouting for him to come
                              won't listen

speeding too fast
down the tracks
no way to slam on the brakes
when I need to/ want to call you baby

once there was a number
but I've forgotten
or the person moved   left no
forwarding
address

hope no body will cross the tracks
all it takes is one split second

from one end of the continent
to the
other

watches gone bananas

they will have to synchronize all the signals
at
green

is there a wall at the end of this
trip
or does one wheel just slip off the tracks real
quick.

What did you expect
stupid
when you committed yourself

> a black guy lookin real cool in a Dashiki
> walked in one nite but when they asked him
> to sign the papers ran right out some of them
> can't take it

did you dream
of a clean white bed
a vase of red roses
white walls with sunlight
cascading
drs. voices murmuring like cool water

you find yourself stripped
stuffed into a striped clown suit

being interviewed by a shrink
sitting on a hard-backed chair
in a large empty room
you speak yr story into a microphone

tape recorded
watched thru a one-way mirror
by six interns on the other side

who need
someone/anyone to study

they can label
cra   zy

> baby they are so glad you happened to drop
> by a mouse in a maze must follow the way
> the walls of the corridors are constructed
> winding around and around can't get out
> til someone plucks.

The Conn. Audubon Society
says it's mating season for frogs
gives a list of various types of frogs
you shd expect to see

this is pg. 73 of today's paper
on pg. 1
a blown up photo of a barge
with fifty women and children
blackened bodies
debris
which
much to the amazement of the bathers
licking ice cream cones
floated in from the sea

on a beach in Vietnam.

In Japan
the trains are so full
speed so fast
at least 100 commuters
try to leap on   get shoved onto the rails
where they fry each morning

on their way to the city
to earn a living.

Later
because you love me
you ask me to tell you

what it was
like

no way to describe

how when you pick up yr favorite book
paragraphs blur together

hands shake too much
to write one word

yr face in the   mirror
split

no way to put it
back
together

                no magic glue and the nurses keep
                saying time and patience

so you sit down on yr cot
stare at yr toes
wait

when they ring the bell
for Occupational Therapy
you go   believe me you go
step by step by step
following bells all day
divides up yr hrs.

you weave the stitches they tell you
make the moccasin that fits no foot
stick hideous pale pink ceramic tiles on ashtrays
clap hands   dance
all the time say yes   yes   yes
to whatever they want

the only way
you get
out   intact.

Seems lately
only place I can be
at my desk

keep hoping if I keep on stitching
black letters together
it will stop the shaking

some things follow you tho
wherever you go

once   remember
in the fall you took me to the mts.
to look at the leaves
night came
looking for a motel
not able to stop

in front of every motel
hanging on a rope from a tree
a dead deer
guts spilled out

red pools I cld drown in

hunting season
it never stops

there was never a room
for lovers like you/me.

The way the crocuses
are suddenly
there
one April morning
                    dark purple petals
                                        opening

hard to believe
every spring
in the same spot
where you first planted those bulbs

new green stems cld shoot up

things can get thru
these terrible
winters
            so can

found poem from Max Cole — WRVR

I'm here every mornin
sometimes I have a
vocabulary
of more than
twenty
words.

Windell Kelly
yes   it's you I'm talking to
locked you in a padded cell
because you heard voices

                    the smart ones walking on Broadway shut up when they
                                                              hear voices

when you tried to tell them
what the voices said
you slurred yr words together so fast
no one cld possibly catch

                    sometimes the words can't keep up with the thoughts

they called you schizo
filled you full of
thorazine
so much medicine you cld swallow buckets of
that purple stuff
all the rooms continued to whirl
lying down all day
yr sweet sweet smile floated over yr bed
listening to yr radio

wake or asleep you wld never move to their bells
follow their schedules
never stop dancing   never stop dancing Windell

                    in OT
                    you refused to stitch their moccasins
                    o how yr sleek hips moved like velvet
                    in the dust filled air amid the sound of
                    shuffling feet old women weeping the broken
                    typewriter they wouldn't let me use

people like that
always use labels
to keep on the other side
what they don't want to/can't
understand

Went by yr house
the other night
all painted white
a For Sale sign
on the grass

looked thru the rooms
all the lights blazing

you had managed to paint it
stick up the sign
before they came to
drag you
off

the clean white paint
flashed on   flashed off
on and off   on and off
saying

        why weren't you here when I needed

Lenore,
you say if someone met you on the street
said nothin but
'Stormy Monday Blues'
you'd get what they mean

either the welfare check
don't come
or their man left
or they is out of a
job

you easily admit
you'd see it different
even speak different   ly
in neat paragraphs
indented five spaces
with all the subjects and verbs in the right places

if you done
lived in a big white house with fifty
rooms   five Cadillacs
up in
Nantucket.

When the station
talk gets interrupted by a long
high-pitched whistle
you have to turn off the radio
get outside
watch the sky

in most countries
they know

the silence
before the planes fly over
the bombs
drop.

Why do all the small animals
keep on fleeing in front of me
frozen in the headlights
                    wherever I go
                            can't get away from those eyes
when I brake it's always too late

even those pills can't stop
altho they make me pretend I'm sleeping

those eyes follow me
down city streets
sit on plates of hot chili
so I can't
even

swallow
the music.

I will go through anything
as long as I can talk

can understand the poet
who said he wished
he cld experience suicide
it wld be
something else to write about

he ended up leaping off the bridge
onto the ice

sometimes you get too close to the fire baby
if you stick in yr little finger

                        you get so mesmerized

can't pull out

I go cra zy
now
only if my ribbon gets twisted.

At least on WRVR
where jazz goes on 22 hrs a day
someone comes in every few hrs
to relieve
the announcer
                     someone can always take the place of Max Cole or
                     Ed Beach

at least there
the records are already cut
neat in shiny jackets
all you got to do is pull one out

line them up on the shelf
make some light amusing patter

here if you shimmy like yr sister Kate
you got to not only shimmy but keep it up
talk about it too.

Do I want these little blue pills to come between me
& my pain

me and my pain
been livin together so long
we're buddies   Mutt and Jeff

my lover wants to know what the pills do
to my head

I tell him it's like the difference between
balancing on the edge of a cliff
thinking any second you're gonna fall off

or still balancing on the edge of the cliff
but forgetting how far down you
cld
fall

how near that edge you actually
walk.

Dear Lyn,

They shower you with silver confetti
flowers

they say
I told you so
when they read yr name in lights

yr old shrink even invites
you for dinner tho
he forgot to leave his forwarding address

last letter says
you're stuck for eight hrs at the Chicago airport
with the flu
taking Coricidin   drugged
sleeping on a bench in the cold terminal on account of blizzards
                                                                and fog

nothing can be predicted   the way it rolls in
planes go up   planes go down   what kind of schedule
at home yr lover criticizes the chipped paint on yr walls

waiting for another check from yr ex

where ever you go
they shower you with silver confetti.

When I write you a letter now
like to time them so they arrive
every six months
just to keep in touch
                    let you know I didn't forget

sign my name in three parts

first name   you never used even when I swallowed those
                                                            pills and
                    was dying

second name   the maiden name you never knew

married name   remember the day you summoned my husband to
                                                        to demand
                    a letter saying you were no longer responsible for
                                                            my life
                    terrified lest you be sued

lines between say
how are you hope you are fine
enclosed is a copy of my latest book yours truly

encased in ice baby
where you can't break thru anymore with yr picks
this kind of ice won't melt even in the hottest tropical
sun

I learned to sit inside nice and cool

removed from
yr glistening lips   yr smile   yr eyes.

I turn the music louder
drown out the reporter's
monotone
telling tales of nine men hanged this morning
two hundred families driven out of their homes by water
blizzards about to hit South Dakota
roads blocked ones who
ones who

can't even get back to where
they
began

never wake
up.

Some of the young ones
have stopped listening to the news

don't even know why tv was invented

don't want to work for IBM
live in the suburbs
with a baby blue station wagon   a washing machine

what's happened to the American dream

all day
they
sing
use pails of chlorox on old blue jeans
make white clouds fly
over the
hips.

The Vietnamese child you hold in yr arms
you want to teach her Friday night to light
candles
like a
real Jewish woman

the lost bells of her people continue
to chime softly

in her blood burnt thatched huts
raped women
children shot in the head
falling   falling into ditches

all those green hills leveled
some songs continue
even tho you
cut off the
singers'
tongues.

Lying on the beach
when the Germans came thru
guns fired   bombs dropped
screams

when I heard the silence
the footsteps
fell down on the sand

played dead
knew if I moved an inch
even flicked an eyelash

I'd be shot in the head
prayed no one wld
flip me over to check

they figured
if I was lying right there in the open
I must be dead
                otherwise I'd be cra zy
                    so baby, they walked right on by
                                        walked right
                                        on by

after a while
got up and took a look
at all the bodies piled up around me

went in for a nice cool swim

this dream reminds me so much
of me/you.

Towards the end
before Virginia walked down to the stream
how fast   how much was she writing

did she try to lie down and rest
did she ever complain to Leonard about her
exhaustion

did she feel like she was living off some kind of crazy speed
that would never stop
did she beg her dr. for pills

did she wake up nights
with paragraphs in her head
the water   the black water flowing
sit up til 6 a.m. to get them down
the way she saw them written
                                    as if by someone else

did she laugh
when someone suggested she
dictate

& that idea of using a heavy stone
a rope
to drag her down

wanting so badly to make sure
once under you never come

you wouldn't think
it wld have even worked in such a shallow
stream   hardly a trickle
                          how I loved that woman.

If you split open an orange
all the juice runs out
a sweet smell
sticks to yr fingers

that dead skunk
smashed into a red ball
on the Taconic

follows me all the way home
even tho I rolled all my
windows
up

when my headlights
hit
him.

No way to tell someone else what it's like
to suddenly
push open
a
door

things locked inside yr room
the key you can't find
is never

mine.

When she drove along the Italian coast
in her bright blue Simca

starving naked children
came crowding around the car

had never seen anything like

whole families
living in holes in the ground since the last war
windows of chicken wire

the clawing hands   cries
made her roll up her windows
lock her
door

not something she cld write home about on a postcard
she came to see
the sea sparkling like soda pop.

When we lived together baby
dreamed I was driving this car
talking   talking to you

when I turned to look
because you were silent
yr stuffing came out in big white tufts
flew off into the wind

nothin but cloth and cotton
button eyes

sewed on with
loose
stitches

alone on a dark rainy street
saying the Lord's prayer
where were . . . .